No Holds Barred Fighting:
Takedowns

Books by Mark Hatmaker

No Holds Barred Fighting:
The Ultimate Guide
to Submission Wrestling

More No Holds Barred Fighting: Killer Submissions

No Holds Barred Fighting: Savage Strikes

Boxing Mastery

No Holds Barred Fighting:
Takedowns

Throws, Trips, Drops and Slams
for NHB Competition and Street Defense

Mark Hatmaker

Photography by Doug Werner

Tracks Publishing
San Diego, California

No Holds Barred Fighting:
Takedowns
Mark Hatmaker

Tracks Publishing
140 Brightwood Avenue
Chula Vista, CA 91910
619-476-7125
trkspub@pacbell.net
www.startupsports.com

Publisher's Cataloging-in-Publication

    Hatmaker, Mark.
      No holds barred fighting : takedowns : throws, trips, drops and slams for NHB competition and street defense / Mark Hatmaker ; photography by Doug Werner.
      p. cm.
      LCCN 2005907146
      ISBN 1-884654-25-8

      1. Hand-to-hand fighting–Handbooks, manuals, etc.
2. Wrestling–Handbooks, manuals, etc.   I. Werner, Doug, 1950- II. Title.

GV1111.H335 2005   796.81
                               QBI05-600135

To my empirical forerunners
whose work knocks me off my feet —
Rakjo Petrov,
M. Briggs Hunt,
Shozo Sasahara
and Ray F. Carson.

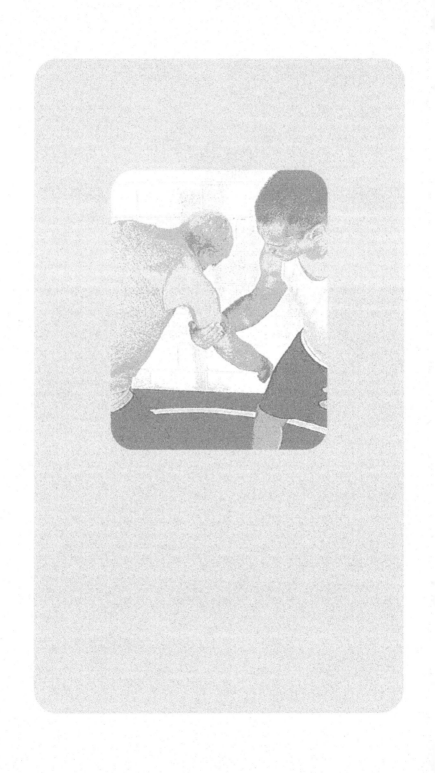

Acknowledgements

Phyllis Carter — editing

Kylie Hatmaker — stage direction

Kory Hays — partner, opponent, grimacer

Jim Montalbano — graphic production

Mitch Thomas — call outs

Preface

You've heard that 90 percent of fights end up on the ground. Well, most all start standing up.

Whether you take it to the ground or stay on your feet, the takedown is a key skill in the combat equation. This go-to manual gives you all you need to know about the formidable skill of shooting (old-school parlance for takedowns). You will learn the best stances for both takedown offense and defense, the footwork peculiar to shooting, "Think Before You Shoot" concepts and dozens of permutations of the highest percentage shots. The latter include double-leg takedowns, single-leg takedowns, snatch singles, low singles and scores of counters.

In short, if you want to gain the takedown in every fight or increase your odds of staying on your feet, this guide has got the goods.

Mark Hatmaker

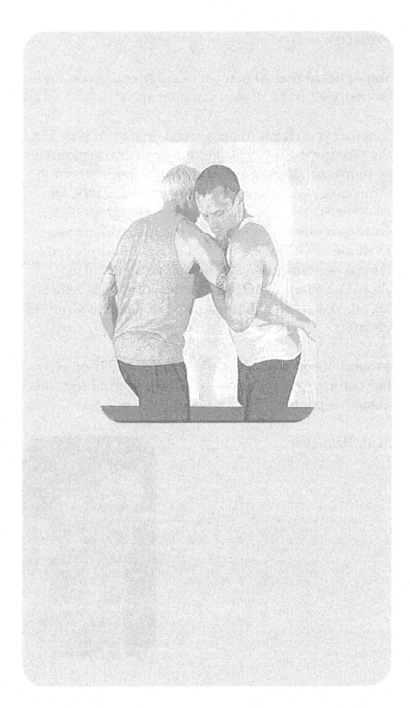

Contents

Warning label
Submission wrestling includes contact and can be dangerous. Use proper equipment and train safely. Practice with restraint and respect for your partners. Drill for fun, fitness and to improve skills. Do not fight with the intent to do harm.

Introduction

Numbers for consideration.

Ninety percent of fights end up on the ground.

And 99.9 percent start standing up (I would say 100 percent, but I've seen more than a few JJ matches in which at least one of the participants starts on his butt).

Eighty-five percent of freestyle wrestling victories can be predicted based upon who scores the first takedown.

The stats bear out the fact that the takedown is an integral part of the game, whether it be NHB, submission wrestling, straight wrestling, jiujitsu or even street defense. The takedown is the key transitional skill between the striking and ground games.

Some people call it bridging the gap. Others call it closing the gap. I've heard one coach refer to it as "the six feet of hell between you and your opponent." In this guide, we call takedowns by the old-school term, "shooting," and individual takedowns, "shots."

I stick with the old-school terminology for two reasons:

● My background is old school, so it's props to the lineage, if you will.

● To my mind, shooting is the perfect metaphor for capturing the skill set necessary to create a good takedown artist — a real sharp shooter.

A sharp shooter realizes that the takedown is not a haphazard grab at his opponent's legs or a fumbling grasp for a quasi-hug/body lock. A sharp shooter realizes, just as his firearms compatriot, that good shooting is about range, target acquisition, muzzle velocity, and, in the case of game shooting, selecting the right caliber weapon for the particular species to be brought down. This book allows you to take the shooting metaphor and build and hone each of the skills to their optimum. Let's load up.

Shot selection

As with all my guides, the shots presented here are not all the possible shots by any stretch of the imagination. Several more volumes would not exhaust the material. I have selected high percentage weapons, run them through common variations that you may encounter in the real-life feedback loop of the fight, and then turned the game around to present intelligent counters to the shots provided.

The takedowns have been culled from several wrestling systems, and all are natural-handle dependent. That means no takedown is an adaptation of a gi or jacketed throwing arts curriculum. The jacketed arts have excellent arsenals of throwing techniques, but the focus on the cloth handle provides a limited transfer to the zero cloth handles of NHB or the flimsy material of street clothing. By limiting all handles to those that are provided by the human body — wrists, neck, upper arms, crotch and so on — we are able to transfer our shooting arsenal to all takedown scenarios, jacketed arts included. The same cannot be said of takedown approaches where the cloth handle is a generous portion of the art.

Most shots featured here are high percentage — the likelihood of using them or being confronted with them is high. But there are smatterings of lower percentage shots that are very effective yet used less frequently because of general unfamiliarity or poor application. This manual will show you how to slip these nasty little surprises into your game with ease.

Clinch work

The clinch. It's an inevitable event at some point in most fights. The ins and outs of clinching deserve detailed coverage. So, out of respect for this formidable aspect of the game we have culled all clinch work from this volume. We will cover that in depth in a separate book — strategy, theory, striking, takedown offense and defense.

Never fear. You are on the right progressive path because you cannot clinch if you cannot shoot. Shoot well and you may bypass the clinch. If you do not — we've got you covered.

Staying on your feet

There is a clear division in the combat arts between strikers and grapplers. This division has grown narrower, but one that needs to be crossed nevertheless. Some adherents of the striking arts have little to zero desire to become master grapplers. Does this mean they have chosen imprudently?

Not necessarily. If a striker eschews all grappling and takedown work and persists in pursuing MMA, a rude awakening is in store. But the MMA striker can make the striking game his mainstay if he adds razor sharp countershooting to his arsenal. With that goal in mind, the striking aficionado can take this guide and inculcate the defensive and counter material as an adjunct to the striking regimen and make more than a decent showing as an MMA athlete. Vanderlai Silva of Pride fame is a masterful testament to this strategy of fantastic sprawling and shot stuffing combined with vicious striking attacks.

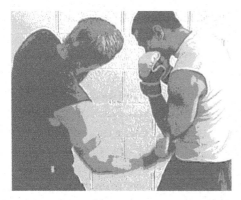

If you decide to use this manual as a takedown defense primer, don't under-estimate the offensive content and move too quickly to the defensive sec-tion. To ignore the offensive mechanics of the takedown is a mistake for the shot stuffer. By understanding the mechanics of proper shooting, the defensive artist can better apply his game in a manner that deliberately undermines the strong aspects of the given shot. Think of it this way — demolition special-ists who bring down buildings with hyper-technical precision can do so because they have an expert grasp of construction engineering, even if they have never actually constructed a building. In other words, to stuff takedowns at the expert level you must understand them inside and out — then you can confidently set yourself to the task of demolishing them.

The missing link

One last item that may seem obvious. Essentially there are only three components to any fight — striking, shooting and grappling. I include the upright clinch in the grappling category. There are unarmed combat fight range theories that postulate four, five, even ten (!) ranges. But let's be pragmatic. Sure there are overlaps, such as striking in the grappling range, but a fight is made up of striking, shooting and grappling. That's it.

Fighters, and fight fans in particular, tend to lump great fighters into one of two camps — strikers and grapplers. Many appreciate a canny shoot when they see it, but for the most part, fighters emphasize one of the two main camps. What is left is the shooting range. This missing link is what separates the two fighting camps. The truth of the matter is that you can't be a master grappler if you can't get your man on the ground. Or as a master striker you may be cutting off some effective striking (the ground and pound game) if you do not know how to drop your opponent and get to tenderizing in the horizontal.

My advice is to give proper weight to all three components, and be careful not to treat shooting as a poor stepchild.

1 Shooting range

Shooting implies that there is a distance to be traversed. All shots are predicated on the fact that you've got to cover some ground to execute the takedown you desire (clinching is a another matter altogether).

Is there a specific distance that is optimum to shoot from? You betcha! As a rule, if you can't touch your opponent — don't shoot. In straight wrestling, you must be able to lay a hand on your opponent before you shoot. In NHB or in the street, the jab acts as the range finder. If your jab does not connect, you are out of range. When the jab finds the mark, it's time to go in.

Side notes

Do not use a kick as your shooting range gauge for two reasons:

● The leg is longer than your arm, and what you may be able to touch with your foot may be the six inches (at the absolute minimum) that gets you in trouble if you shoot.

● Shooting is about speed. Using your leg as a range finder assumes you've got time to get that same leg back underneath your hips for proper driving. That's asking too much.

This is not an argument against kicking, but an argument against using the kick as an immediate precedent to the shoot.

Why can't I shoot if I can't touch my opponent?

Remember when you first started punching and were told not to telegraph a punch? It's easy to tip your opponent to your punching intentions by merely dipping a shoulder or providing some other tell with a single limb (not even the largest limb at that). Imagine how easy it is to read an entire body making its way toward you. That's why you must be as close as possible before shooting. We've got to stack the deck in our favor with every trick we can cobble.

One more time — if you can't touch your opponent, don't shoot.

2 Shooting stances

In standard wrestling, there are the square and staggered stances. But to take into consideration the striking component of NHB and self-defense, we need something a little different. Not much different, mind you. We'll gladly keep what works. The

NHB shooting stance is the standard modified boxing stance (for a detailed description of this stance see the book, *No Holds Barred Fighting: Savage Strikes*). For submission wrestling, either the square or the staggered stance will work, but I advocate a staggered stance variant for the following reasons.

Most combat athletes today cross-train in submission wrestling (no striking) and NHB (striking included). It's wise to have a stance that blends easily between the two without feeling you're playing at two different mind-sets.

The modified staggered stance affords better defense against shooting and submission setups.

Standard staggered stance

● The staggered stance as used in freestyle wrestling, begins with the legs approximately shoulder width apart.

● The lead foot steps forward approximately a step and a half.

● The knees are bent.

● The body bends forward at the waist, while the back is kept relatively straight.

Important — Do not allow your shoulders to penetrate the invisible vertical plane traveling skyward from your lead knee. To allow the shoulders to drift beyond this plane provides easy opportunities for your opponent to unbalance you and/or snap you to the mat.

● The rear hand is placed on the rear knee to provide protection against shots to this leg.

● The lead elbow is placed on the lead knee with the palm facing up. Positioning the hand in this manner protects the lead leg.

This stance has a low base and provides deep stability. Moving the arms into underhook position makes them ready to defend upper and lower body takedowns. Drawbacks are obvious. In the striking match, the head is wide open. The legs are too far apart to afford the rapid mobility needed to evade a speedy and vicious leg-kicker. This stance is ideal for the straight wrestling match and perhaps for the submission match, but it's bad news for the NHB player.

Modified staggered stance

This is the stance I advocate for the NHB player who desires to cross-train in the submission only game. It allows you to blend the two games with a minimum of adjustments. You will notice that it is only slightly different from the standard striking stance but uses some of its components.

● The legs are shoulder width apart.

● The lead leg is placed one natural step forward. The more upright position provides greater mobility.

● Both elbows are kept close to the body to prevent underhooking and arm dragging.

● The lead hand drops approximately 12 inches below your chin with the palm up.

● The rear hand turns palm down and is placed approximately 12 inches forward of the rear shoulder. As a visual mnemonic, imagine holding a large invisible medicine ball between your two palms — the lower palm up, the rear palm down.

● The back is held somewhat straight with a bit of forward lean, but not as extreme as in the standard staggered stance.

Drill notes

From this position, you should be able to drop immediately into the standard staggered stance if the need arises. As a matter of fact, I recommend drilling that movement extensively. Move from the modified staggered stance to the standard staggered stance before a mirror. Then drill it with a partner who shoots a double leg that you defend by dropping to the standard staggered stance.

A note on hand placement

The lead hand can drift forward or to the rear, but always think of it being directed at a spot just below

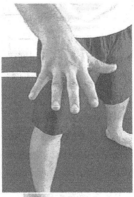

your opponent's chin. Placing your lead hand to the outside of this position opens the legs. Thinking "hand under chin" provides many defensive opportunities. Drilling this will confirm it.

Finger safety

Thumbs out, fingers together. Splayed fingers are easily broken or jammed. Breaks come from an opponent slapping at a hand to catch your wrist or jamming them on the way in. Keep your fingers together. You don't have to squeeze them tight. Leaving the thumb out will provide all the grip power you need.

Think like a sprinter

Traditional martial arts are fond of T-stances. The theory is that the body presented sideways offers a smaller target. Chances are you have already seen more than enough empirical examples of myths being shattered when the traditional meets the pragmatic in NHB competition. The traditional arts have their place, but it's not in the confines of hybrid reality fighting.

The T-stance is anathema to the savvy shooter. Structurally, it's all wrong. The feet are pointing in two different directions. In order to make any speedy or powerful transfer of your body weight toward the direction you wish to shoot, first you've got to align the skeletal structure of your legs to your target or desired direction of movement. Some will argue that you can shove off the rear foot that is pointed perpendicular to your target. That can be done, but again at the expense of maximum speed and optimum power.

Optimum foot placement for moving in any given direction is to have the feet and knees facing the direction you wish to travel. This is how we walk and run. It is no different in positioning our feet for shooting. For a superlative example of what works for exceptional initial speed, look to Olympic-class sprinters. When they position themselves in the blocks, they align the feet, the knees and the entire body toward the direction they wish to move.

Nose on

Here's a Western scientific axiom that has an Eastern correlate. Keep your nose on your opponent's centerline. What does this mean? It means what it says. Look at your opponent, yourself or any human being. Observe that humans have bilateral symmetry. If a body is split down the middle, you have a mirror image of each half. These halves conjoin in an imaginary line that can be drawn down the center of our bodies from the top of the head to the groin.

To keep your nose on an opponent means to always face your nose on his centerline, no matter the distance between you. By going nose on, you ensure that you keep your body square to your opponent. This allows proper alignment for rapid shooting and easy access to all your offensive and defensive tools.

Off line

This rule is the converse of nose on. Your primary goal is to keep nose on with your opponent. Your secondary goal is to get your opponent to face off line. To face off line means to outmaneuver, outclass, or feint your opponent off his nose-on position. When you make your opponent face off your centerline, you will expose an entire side of his body vulnerable to attack. The off line can be subtle or conspicuous. Your job as a top shooter is to exploit every off-line opportunity, and this is done only with complete observation of staying nose on.

That's a lot to think about for a stance, huh? Drill all facets in a mirror or with a partner until they are natural. Change levels, change leads. Now it's time to move.

3 Shooting footwork

Below are the rules of movement found in all of our texts. I don't usually repeat myself because I intend for each volume to be an interlocking piece of a greater whole, but it's probably wise to go over this one more time.

Rule one
Whatever direction you wish to move, move the foot that is closest to that direction first.

Rule two
Step and drag. Keep your feet close to the mat. Don't lift them. To do so provides an opportunity to be swept or caught on a one-legged base.

Rule three
Maintain your base. Don't cross your feet and keep them a shoulder's width apart while moving.

Rule four
Have a fluid shift step. To shift step, step the lead foot to the rear or the rear foot to the lead, landing in perfect stance. Drill both variations until they are smooth.

Rule five

Be fluid in all eight directions of movement as indicated by this diagram.

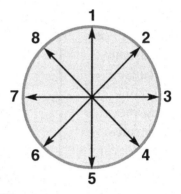

Footwork drills

Begin at the center of this figure facing number one. Run a few rounds moving through each of the following footwork patterns.

1. Advance to one — lead foot moves first.

2. Retreat to five — rear foot moves first.

3. Sidestep to three — in a right lead, the lead foot moves first. Left lead, the rear foot moves first.

4. Sidestep to seven — right lead moves the rear foot first. Left lead moves the lead foot first.

5. Advance to two — right lead moves the lead foot. Left lead shift steps.

6. Advance to eight — right lead shift steps. Left lead moves the lead foot.

7. Retreat to four — right lead shift steps. Left lead moves the rear foot.

8. Retreat to six — right lead moves rear foot first. Left lead shift steps.

Penetration steps versus leg dives

If you are close enough to clinch, there is not much call to ponder how you got there. If you can't touch your opponent, there is much to consider. There are two schools of thought on how to close this distance and each school comes from Western wrestling. These schools can be called the Penetration Step School and the Leg Dive School, or New School and Old School. A detailed breakdown on the two and a brief subjective commentary on which is "better" follows.

So which is better? The answer sounds like a hedge, but it's honest — the school that works best for you in a particular situation is the winner. I use both schools with about 25 percent more weight toward the Leg Dive. I find that Old School is more sound for defense in the All-in/NHB game and less likely to telegraph intention. I admit a prejudice for Old School, so keep in mind that the last comment is purely subjective. I use both schools and have seen numerous New School shooters use the penetration step exclusively with fantastic success. It is smart to explore both trains of thought and allow athletes to decide for themselves which school they spend the majority of their time pursuing.

Pay attention to each school because once we hit the takedown curriculum, we move directly to the setup and drop portion of the technique. The entry is up to you. You'll see both schools in the photos.

New School / penetration step
New School wrestling has seven basic skills: stance and movement, penetration step, lifting, hip heist, back arch, back step and coming to base. All golden skills, indeed. Here we concentrate on the penetration step.

● Hit your stance.

● With most of your weight over your lead foot, drop your base by bending at the knees.

● Drive off your trail foot and step your lead foot between or past your opponent's feet on the outside as far as you can manage without sacrificing base.

Breaking the glass concept
Imagine a vertical pane of glass that is directly behind your opponent's heels. Always strive to break this pane of glass with your penetration step. By "breaking the glass" you ensure that you have adequately penetrated your opponent's base.

Penetration step with backstep
This variation allows for a stronger drive, but you must

Penetration step with backstep

Penetration step "banging the knee"

be artful and thoroughly committed because this addition is a huge telegraph.

● It's like the preceding move, you begin by moving your rear foot directly underneath your hips. This allows you to have a stronger drive position.

● As you reposition your rear foot, hit your level change simultaneously.

Penetration step "banging the knee"

It is preferable to stay on your feet for single- and double-leg drives. However, if an opponent maneuvers toward the retreat range (his five, your one) or you desire a quick drop out of range, the knee bang is an acceptable alternative.

● Use either of the trail foot drive positions described before.

● Shoot while dropping your base.

● The lead knee, instead of the lead foot, breaks the glass and you should pop up immediately.

Two knee banging rules

● Spend as little time on your lead knee as possible.

● Strive to bang only the lead knee. Getting caught with two knees down puts you in an inferior position.

4 Old School leg dives

These are subtle moves and learning them is easier than it may first appear. Following are a solo drill, three ways to hit the leg dive (notice the leg is not picked up since we're just showing how to hit the dive itself) and finally, one position for recovery after a thwarted leg dive.

Solo dive

The dive is just what it sounds like — a dive into the mat.

● Hit your stance and imagine yourself standing at the edge of a swimming pool.

● Moving your hands before your upper body, reach for the water as if you were diving.

● As you dive, break your body into chain links — the hands move first, then the head and finally the waist.

● With the palms of your hands, slap the mat directly in front of the toes of your lead foot.

Get comfy with this breaking of the body into chain links and make a total commitment to the dive to your toes.

Double-leg dive

● Dive at your opponent's legs without moving your feet using the chain link manner of movement.

● From a right lead and with total commitment, dive at your opponent's right lead. Aim your head to the outside of his right knee.

● Allow your right shoulder to impact on top of his right thigh. This move will stop your dive.

Important

● Do not control your descent — allow his body to break your fall.

● Place your hands behind his knees.

● Once your shoulder bangs into him, step your rear foot forward.

Old School leg dives

Single-leg dives — head to the outside, two views

Single-leg dive — head to the outside
● Dive as described in the double leg aiming for his right leg lead.

● Allow your shoulder to impact his thigh.

● Your lead hand goes behind his lead knee.

● The rear hand reaches for his lead heel.

● As in the previous move (and all leg dives for that matter) the rear foot moves after the dive.

Single-leg dive — head to the inside
● Hit your standard dive but move your head to the inside of his lead leg.

● Impact your rear shoulder on his thigh.

● Place your rear hand behind his knee.

● Lead hand cups the heel.

● The rear foot can now step forward.

At this point, I'm sure you've noticed a pattern to the hand placement. Let's spell it out.

Two rules of single-leg dive hand positioning:
● One hand is high (knee); one hand is low (heel).

● The side your head is nearest indicates which hand reaches for the heel.

Single-leg dive — head to the inside, two views

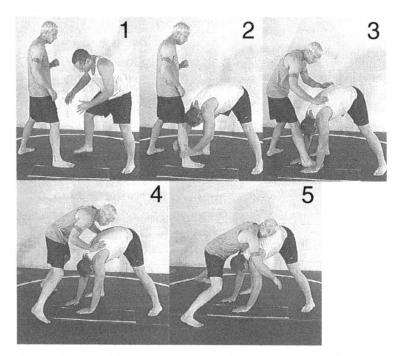

Leg dive recovery

As you can see, if your opponent causes you to miss your leg dive, you will wind up in a three-point base that resembles the end point of the solo leg-dive drill. No problem. Immediately spring up and return to stance. Notice in the photos that even if your opponent sprawls at this point, your hips are high, and you will have zero problem hitting him with a wing or duck-under to escape or gain top position.

There you have it — Old School and New School. I urge you to drill both school entries and become proficient in each.

Hands on

Once you close the distance, you've got to know how to get hold of your opponent. Keep the following concepts in mind.

Hit him where he bends

Joints are the primary structural weakness in the human skeleton. The body is more apt to collapse at joints than at bone. Play to that natural fact and strive to place your hands and body at joints — otherwise known as hitting him where he bends.

We use the double-leg takedown to illustrate this point.

● When hitting the double leg, I place both my hands behind his knees (no higher, no lower).

● I place my shoulder in his waist (another bending joint).

● By hooking him at his joints, I have better control over him if he sprawls.

With incorrect form — gripping too high or too low on his legs — his countering sprawl still can be implemented with relative ease.

Wedges

Wedges are parts of the body that provide good control over your opponent's center of mass. There are two primary centers of mass in the human body — the chest and the hips.

There are many minor wedges, but the two major ones that you need to understand are the high crotch and the armpits. These wedges are susceptible to deep underhook placement, therefore prime for control.

The photo of Kory shows the three main wedge targets on a body.

5 Handles

Handles are body parts that can be gripped for better control over your opponent as you set him up for a takedown. The following handles are useful for various takedowns and can be combined in myriad ways. With a partner, run through the following handles till you commit them to muscle memory.

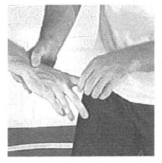

Finger grab
Grab all four of your opponent's fingers. Old School wrestling emphasizes finger grabbing over wrist holds for a good reason. Fingers provide you with much more control.

Safety note — all or none
Fingers snap easily. When grabbing your opponent's fingers, the rule is all or none. This means that if you can't grab all four fingers at once, don't grab any. In the street it's all in, but for drilling and competition, play it like gentlemen.

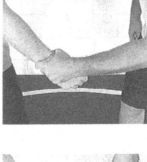

Outside one-on-one
Grip the back of your opponent's wrist with one hand.

Inside one-on-one
Grip the inside of your opponent's wrist with one hand.

Two-on-one
Grab your opponent's wrist with both hands

The following four body locks can be hit from front or rear.

Palm-to-palm body lock
Grip your hands in a palm-to-palm grip around your opponent's body.

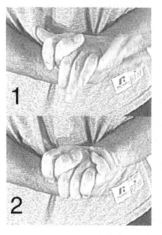

Three finger grip body lock
Insert your right thumb between the index and middle finger of your left hand and grip your fingers. This grip is stronger than the standard palm to palm because of the smaller circumference of the grip.

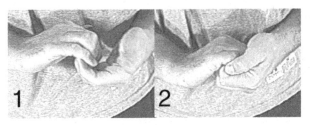

Finger hook grip body lock
Form the ends of your fingers into hooks and interlock.

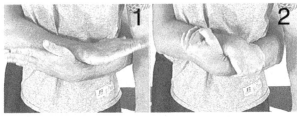

Butterfly grip
Each hand grasps the inner wrist of the other hand.

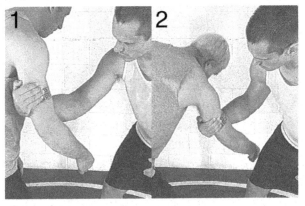

Arm drag
Your right hand overhooks your opponent's right triceps. Pull his arm across his body 45 degrees and down.

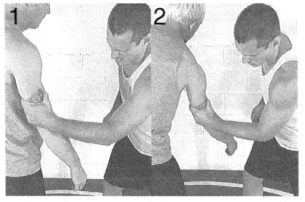

Cross drag

Your left hand overhooks your opponent's right triceps. Pull his arm across his body 45 degrees and down.

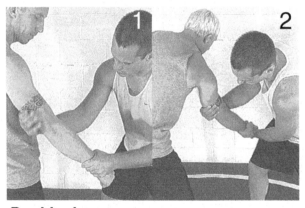

Double drag

Grip his right wrist with your left hand. Grip his right triceps with your right hand. Pull his arm across his body 45 degrees and down.

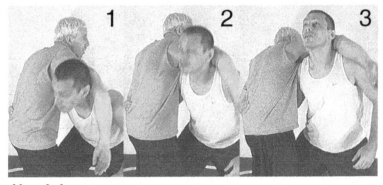

Head drag
Underhook his armpit wedge with the back of your head. Arch your back.

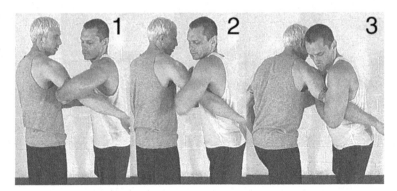

Single overhook
Overhook his right arm above the elbow with your left arm.

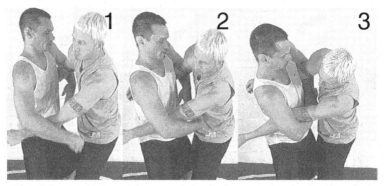

Double overhook

Overhook both his arms above the elbows with your arms.

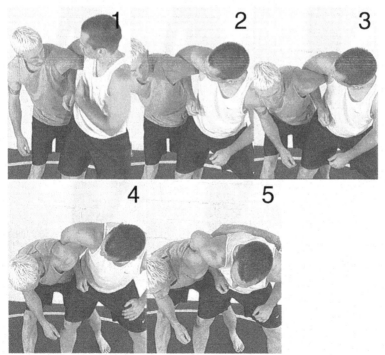

Whizzer

Overhook his right arm at the armpit with your left arm.

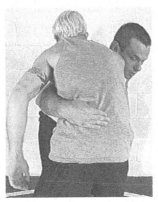

Waist chancery
Grip his waist at the beltline with your right arm. Waist chanceries can be applied from the front or the back.

Single head hook
Overhook his neck with the crook of your right arm.

Headlock hook
Set your single head hook. Grip your hands together.

Thigh overhook
Overhook his right thigh at the knee with your left hand.

Thigh underhook
Underhook his right thigh at the knee with your left hand.

Two grips to avoid

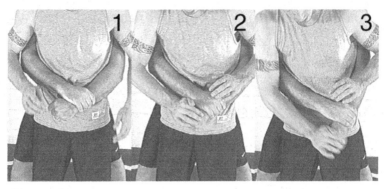

Bar grip

Grab your own left wrist with your right hand. This grip allows your opponent to easily peel off your protruding left hand.

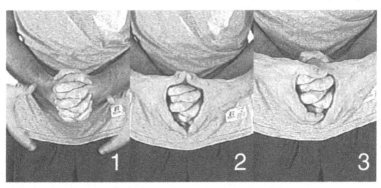

Fingers interlocked grip

This grip leads to broken fingers. You either will be wrenched during movement or your opponent will overgrip your fingers and squeeze to cause pain or break them.

Now that the vast majority of preliminaries have been reviewed we're almost ready to go. Setups are next, and then it will be time to start dropping your man.

6 Setups

A setup is a move that offsets your opponent's base or distracts him from the fact that you are about to hurl your body's mass at him. In All-In/NHB, striking (primarily the jab) is the setup of practical choice, but in straight submission (and if the opportunity presents itself in All-In/NHB) many of the following will be of use.

Numerous setups are presented and I suggest you work them as diligently as you do takedowns. The takedowns in this book, like these setups, are not all that are available, but are enough to get your game up to respectable snuff.

Head snap
Aggressively pull ("snap") your opponent's head down.
As he resists, shoot in.

5 *Head pressure*
Apply downward pressure to his head. When you feel him fight his head up, release his head and shoot.

Head shove
Push his head. When he resists, shoot.

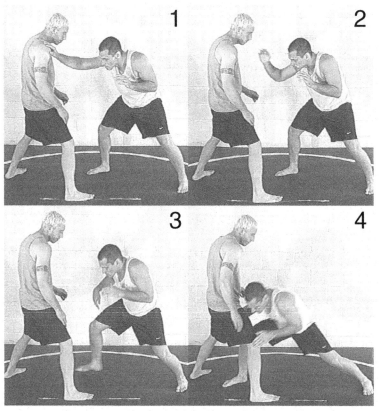

Shoulder tap
Tap (shove) his shoulder a few times to get him accustomed to the action. Fake a tap and shoot.

Shoulder pop

Your opponent is holding onto your elbow. Shove his shoulder with your controlled arm and shoot.

Shrug from collar and elbow

Here you are in a collar and elbow tie-up. If he is controlling your neck with his right hand, drive your left shoulder toward his left shoulder while snapping your head out of the way. Shoot.

Shrug from collar and elbow
Another view.

Shuck from collar and elbow

If his right arm is controlling your head, turn your head away from his control arm (not your body).

While turning, use the web of your left hand to drive his right arm across your body. Shoot.

5 ***Elbow press***
Push hard against his elbow. When he pushes back, release his elbow and shoot.

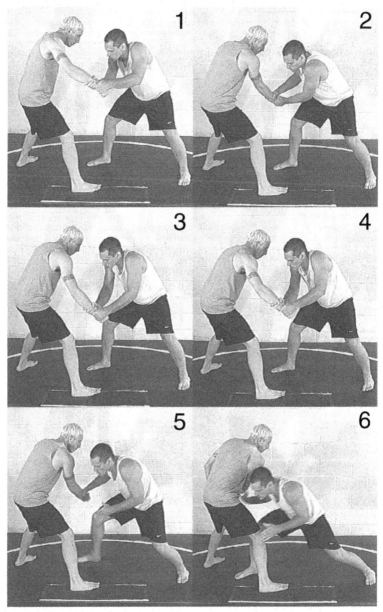

Two-on-one

Grip his arm in a two-on-one. Clear the arm and shoot.

5 *Forearm pull from collar and elbow*

His right arm is controlling your head. Pull on his right forearm with your left hand. Shoot as he resists.

1

2

3

4

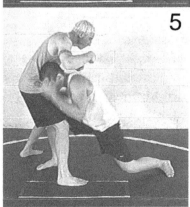

5 **Upper arm pull from collar and elbow**
Pull on his head-control upper arm. Shoot as he resists the action.

Forearm post from collar and elbow

Grip his head-control elbow and keep it stationary and shoot.

5 **_Fake drag_**
Hook an arm drag. As your opponent resists by pulling his arm, release it and shoot.

Elbow teeter-totter from biceps ride
Grip both of his biceps in a biceps ride. Swing one of his arms down and the other up. Shoot under the up arm.

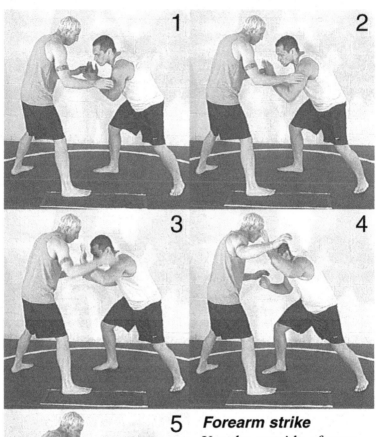

Forearm strike
Use the outside of your forearms to strike his inner arms away from his nose-on line. Shoot.

5 *Double strike*
Strike both his arms to the outside with your forearms. Shoot down the middle.

Forearm pop from collar and elbow

Bring your left arm under his head-control right arm. Use your forearm to strike his arm upward. Shoot.

5 ***Slap out***
Slap his wrist to the outside as you shoot.

Slap in
Slap his wrist to the inside as you shoot.

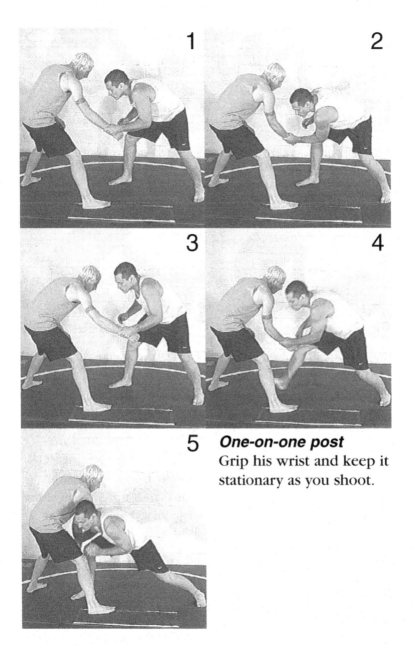

5 ***One-on-one post***
Grip his wrist and keep it
stationary as you shoot.

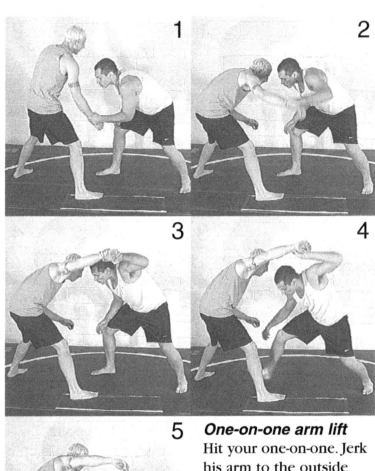

5 ***One-on-one arm lift***
Hit your one-on-one. Jerk
his arm to the outside
and then up. Shoot under
his raised arm.

Double wrist control arm lift

Grab each of his wrists in a one-on-one control. Move his arms to the outside and then up. Shoot.

5 ***Double elbow lift***
Lift both elbows and
shoot underneath them.

Double elbow post
Grip both elbows. Keep them stationary as you shoot.

5 *Double wrist pull*

Grip each of his wrists in a one-on-one. Pull on his wrists. As he resists, shoot.

Chaining setups

Setups in wrestling are just like setups in boxing —
they are more effective in combination. Two setup
combinations follow.

Setup combo #1

Hit the double wrist lift. If this move is successful,
shoot. If the opponent pulls them back to his body,
release one of his wrists, hit an arm drag and then
shoot.

Touch and go
This is a feinting combination. Shove his head. Shove his shoulder. Shoot.

Using these setups and chaining them together will take you to the next level and beyond.

Let's get to dropping.

Takedowns

7
Double-leg takedowns

This is far and away the most prevalent shot attempted. There are numerous ways to follow up the initial shot. Here are some high percentage plays.

Double-leg takedown

● Use either the penetration or leg dive entry. Keep your elbows close to your body when you shoot. Do not reach out. If you do, you may be underhooked and turned.

● Keep your head tight to his body with no gap between your head and his hip. A free head may be hooked into a possible submission attempt.

● Continue your forward momentum while sucking his knees to you.

● Use your head to hook him to the side opposite your head placement. In this case, my head is hooking Kory to my right.

● Once you acquire a takedown, blanket your man immediately. To blanket is to secure the best riding position attainable at that moment.

Double leg from the knees

- Your setup is identical to the preceding move.

- Bang the lead knee to the mat penetrating the heel line. Finish as before.

Double leg with back trip

● Two scenarios — you shoot for the double leg but find yourself unable to bring him down or you shoot with this technique from the start.

● Once you have observed proper technique and banged the lead penetrating knee to the mat, step your trail foot (rear foot) behind his lead leg.

● You will be heel to heel at this point. In this example, the back of my left heel is hooked behind the back of Kory's right

heel.
● Continue your drive to complete the takedown.

● Important — Once you drop him, do not merely lay your hips on his trapped leg because he can scramble out of this position. Strive to turk his leg. To turk is to arch his leg toward the sky by lifting his trapped leg with your leg.

7.1
Double-leg takedown counters

Since this is the number one shot — the jab of the game, if you will — you must have several answers. These aren't all the counters but more than enough for the seasoned player.

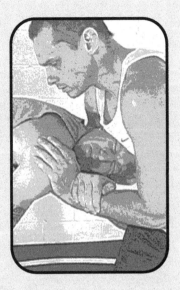

Sprawl

● This is the simplest and most useful double-leg counter.

● To sprawl, launch your legs away from your body and drive your hips into the back of your opponent's head.

● At the bottom of the sprawl, keep your insteps on the mat so that if he continues to drive into you, you are not driven back to your feet. You can be, if you sprawl with the balls of your feet dug into the mat.

● It's vital that you keep your hips driving through your opponent and do not lay your chest on him. Doing so provides him with numerous counter opportunities.

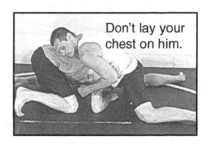

Don't lay your chest on him.

Post chancery

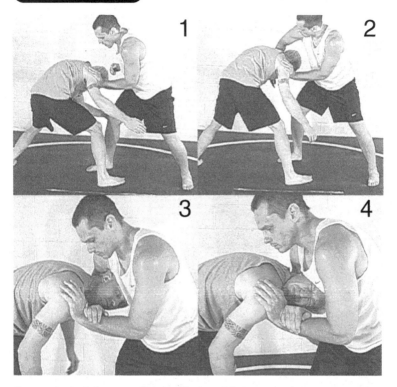

I'm no fan of the standing guillotine. My reasons are covered in *No Holds Barred Fighting: Killer Submissions*. This move and the next two will serve you far more effectively.

● Overhook his head with your right arm.
● Post on his right shoulder with your left hand.
● Keeping his head in the center of your chest, drive your right inner forearm across his face. This can be his throat, jaw,

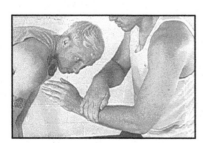

cheek, nose or eye. It's not a picky move. It all hurts.
● Grip your posted left lower forearm with your right hand.
● Drop your base, squeeze your elbows together and gooseneck your right wrist up to tap.

Double-leg takedown counters

Hook chancery

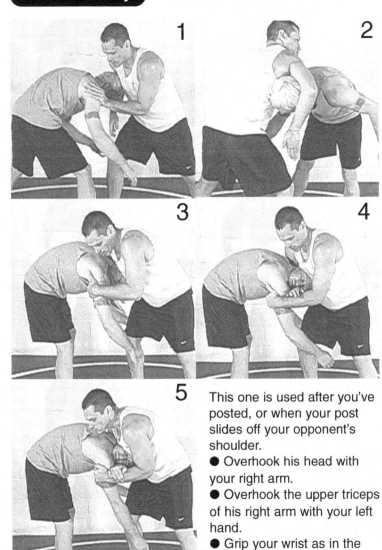

This one is used after you've posted, or when your post slides off your opponent's shoulder.
● Overhook his head with your right arm.
● Overhook the upper triceps of his right arm with your left hand.
● Grip your wrist as in the preceding move.
● Finish as in the post chancery but pull his right upper arm.

Underhook and inside thigh block

1

2

● Remain on your feet in this double-leg block.

● As he drives into you, drop your legs back a bit and underhook one of his shoulders.

● Place your other hand along the inside of his opposite thigh. In this case, I have underhooked Kory's right shoulder with my left arm and blocked his left thigh with my right arm.

● Keeping the pressure on with your hands in this position effectively jams his takedown attempt.

Cross-face and rear crotch

● You initially stay on your feet in this block.

● As he shoots, cross-face your opponent. The inside blade of my left forearm runs underneath his face and then the left hand grips him at his right shoulder.

● Keep the cross-face hooked, turn the corner to hook a rear crotch hold by overhooking his crotch and reach deep into his hips.

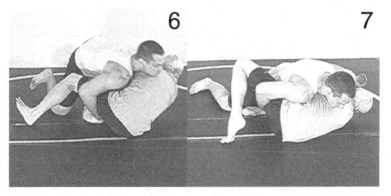

● Maintain your grip and drive into him with your chest to turn him.

● This unseemly looking hold can be used not only to turn him but also to gain a blanket ride.

Cross-face bar

● Hit a cross-face with your left arm.
● Place the elbow of your right forearm on his left scapula.
● Grip your hands and while keeping the pressure on both the cross-face and the elbow, dig in the back, wheel him to your right to face away from you.
● As you perform the wheel, lower your base, This drops him to the mat on his butt.
● Keeping your grip, place the back of his head on your chest.
● Lean forward at the waist and dig your cross-face inner wrist into and up your opponent's face to finish.

Front quarter nelson

● Stuff his head with your right hand. To stuff is to post onto your opponent's head and drive down.
● As you stuff, turn the corner to your left and overhook his right arm with your left arm.

● Figure-4 grip your hands and turn your opponent to the mat using your reinforced figure-4 grip to stuff his head. Lift upward on his right arm with your left arm and back-step with your right foot.

Flat crank

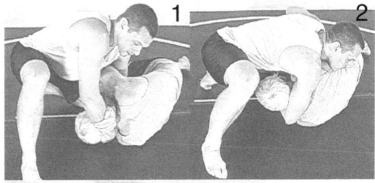

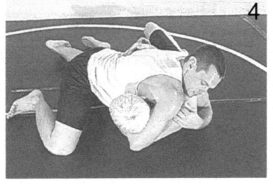

When you hit the mat, there are hundreds if not thousands of submission possibilities. Some high percentage moves follow.

● Once you've dumped him on the mat and covered him in a cross-body ride, encircle and tightly secure his head with your right arm.

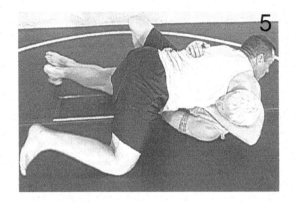

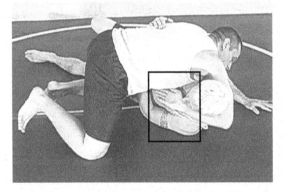

● Arch your hips through him while turning your right shoulder upward. Look over your right shoulder to tap.

Chin hook crank

● This is another possibility from the same front quarter nelson dump.

● Your right arm encircles his head like in the previous technique, but this time, reach all the way around his head to grip his chin with your right hand.

● Use your left hand to underhook his far arm and grip him at the shoulder to stabilize him.

● Hold his chin tightly as you sit out onto your left hip facing the crown of his head to tap.

Reverse half nelson

● A reverse half is essentially a front quarter variant.

● The opponent's head is stuffed with the right hand just like the front quarter.

● Overhook his right arm with your left as in the front quarter.

● Here's the difference — run the underhooking left arm across the back of his head and remove your right hand.

● Perform the same backstep to dump him to the mat.

Princeton bar

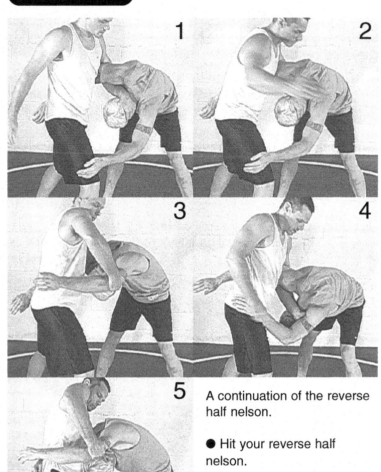

A continuation of the reverse half nelson.

● Hit your reverse half nelson.

● Grab his left triceps with your right hand and transfer it to your left reverse nelson hand.

● Grip and pull his left triceps while cranking his head down to tap.

Double underhook

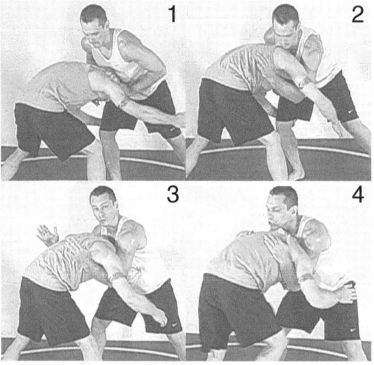

● Underhook his arms at the armpits.

● While doing so, keep the back of his head centered on your chest to prevent him from ducking out to either side and turning you.

● This is a great control/standing ride position. It has the potential to be a submission if you can drive your hips through the back of his head forcing his chin toward his chest.

Double-leg takedown counters

Double underhook to elevator and top-saddle sit-out stocks

● This variant of the previous move should be hit if your opponent gets his head ducked out on either side.

● Once his head is ducked out, keep your underhooks in place.

● Drop your butt to the mat while placing an elevator (an instep) into the inner thigh on the same side of the duckunder.

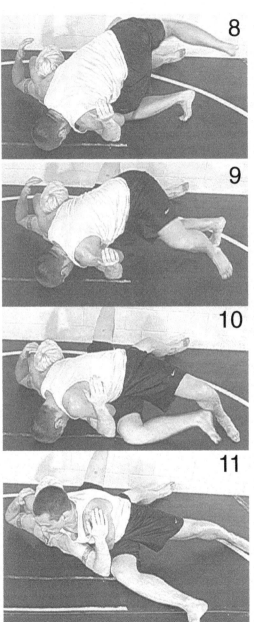

8

9

10

11

● Example —
Kory has ducked
out to my right side
(his left) so I place
my right elevator
underneath his left
thigh. I turn him to
his right (my left)
by kicking upward
with my elevator
and wrench him
toward my left with
my underhooks.
● Important —
The attempt to ele-
vate an opponent
toward his duck-
under side may
allow him to use
his head to post on
the mat and stall or
counter your move.
● Once he is on
his back, keep the
underhooks in
place and his head
under your arm.
● Sit out on the
side opposite his
head. In this case, I
sit out on Kory's
right side.
● Keeping the
underhooks tight,
slide your hips in
the direction of the
crown of his head
to tap.

Double bar arm lock

● This is another double underhook variant.

● Hit the hook-up as in the previous move but strive to grip your hands behind his back.

● With a combination of hips through the back of his head and a tight squeeze on his trapped arms, you may gain a tap if not a damn solid standing ride.

Double bar with back leg trip

● Another double underhook variant in which the opponent ducks his head out to a side.
● In this duckunder counter you opt not to drop to the mat.
● Keep your underhooks tight and hit him with a back heel on the opposite side of his duckunder.

● Example — If he ducks his head out on your right side, you will trip on the far side. He ducks right, you place the back of your right heel behind his right heel and use your underhooks to wrench him to the mat.

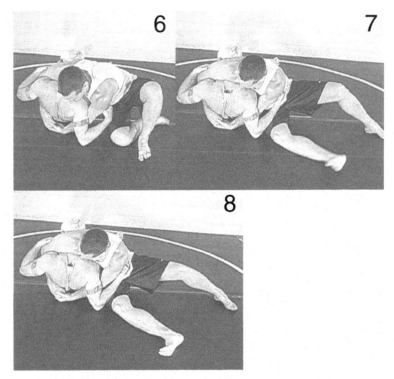

● Once you hit the mat, you may use the sit-out stocks as described in the first double underhook.

Whizzer

● The whizzer is easy to hit when your opponent is reaching wide during his take-down attempts.

● To whizzer, overhook one of his arms with yours. In this sequence, my left versus Kory's right.

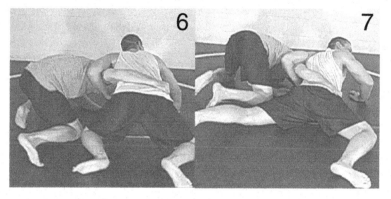

● Drive your whizzer shoulder to the mat while turning away from your opponent.

Whizzer and ankle pickup

● Your opponent may attempt to travel with you after you set your whizzer. The following techniques address your secondary moves.

● Hook you whizzer and then bend at the waist. Reach between your legs and grab and lift his near ankle to drop him to the mat.

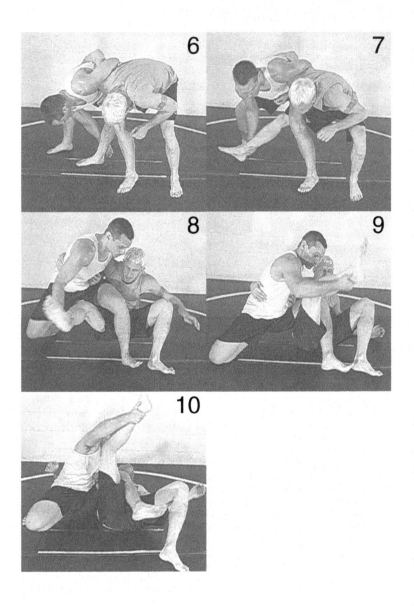

Whizzer with grapevine for fall back

● This is a very effective drop but tough to hit with kindness.

● Hook your whizzer and then inside grapevine his near leg with your near leg.

● Example — If you whizzer with your left arm, grapevine his right leg with your left leg.

● Kick his grapevined leg forward while hitting a back arch over your whizzer shoulder to drop him brutally to the mat.

● Be sweet to your partners on this one. It's a hard drop.

Whizzer throw with inside grapevine and far elbow

● Once you've hooked the grapevine, you may find yourself unable to get enough base to back arch, or, more honestly, you may be a bit cautious about the fall.

● Set the whizzer and inside grapevine, but add a grip to his free arm just above the elbow with your free arm.

● Pull that elbow tight across his body. Then kick your grapevining leg backward to make you both tumble to the mat with you on top.

● Again, this and the previous drop are punishing to your opponent. Play nicely.

Bar arm and chancery

This is an underhook variant.

● Here you are able to underhook an arm and over-hook his head. This is a mighty sweet position to be in.

● To drop, leave your hooks in place, back step away from the side his head is on and wrench him to the mat.

Another view and taking him down

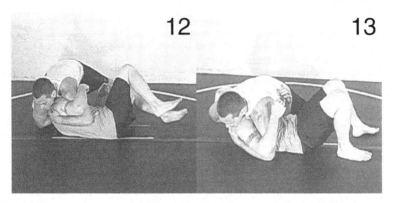

● You can follow with a slew of hooks, but the flat crank and chin hook crank (described on page 110) work beautifully. They are shown next.

Flat crank

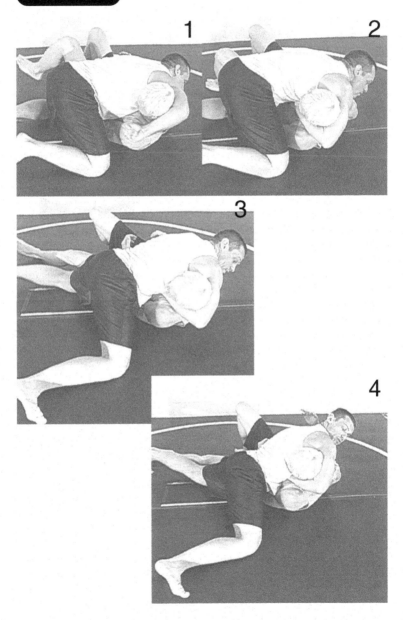

Chin hook crank

Front headlock crank / maximum crank

● Overhook your opponent's head with your right arm. Here it travels under your armpit instead of in the center of the chest, which is optimum.
● Overhook his right arm just above the elbow with your left arm.

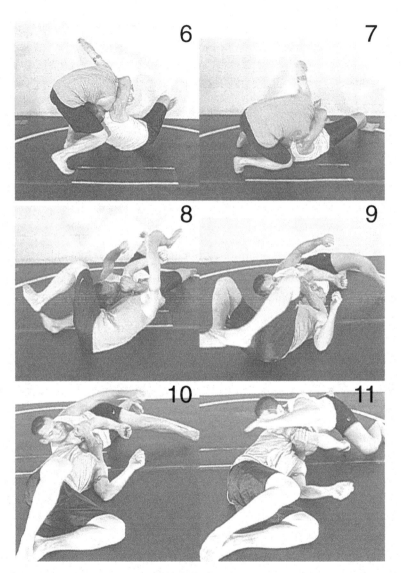

● Grip your hands together.
● Duck your head under the right side of his chest. Barrel roll underneath him. Bring him over the top of you onto his back with you on top.

● During the roll, transition your right hand to a chin hook.
● Keeping his chin gripped, sit out on your left hip facing his head to tap.

Missed maximum crank to naked chin hook roll

- Overhook your opponent's head as in the previous move.
- He fights your attempts to overhook his right arm.
- Hook his chin with your right hand.

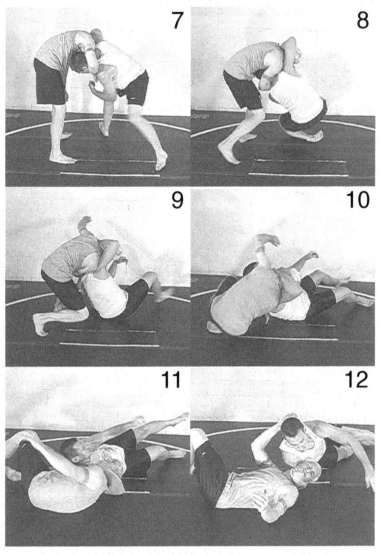

● Duck your head under his right arm.
● Barrel roll underneath him to your left pulling him over you with your chin hook.
● Keeping your chin hook, sit out toward his head to tap.

Finishing from another angle

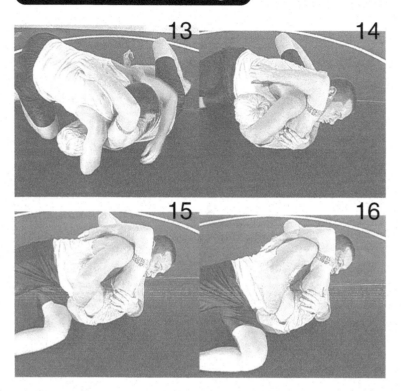

Cross-face and far ankle

● When your opponent shoots, hook a cross-face and drop your base.

● When your opponent hits his knees, turn the corner away from the direction he is facing. Use your free arm to grab his far ankle.

● Keep your hooks in place. Drive your chest through him to turn him.

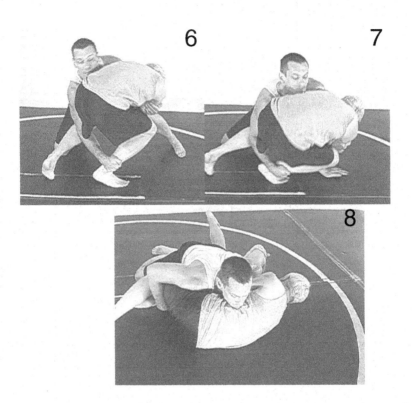

Cross-face and near ankle

- If your opponent's legs are spread so that you cannot reach the more effective far ankle, snatch the near ankle and drive him over.

Crotch lift

- You have sprawled, but your opponent, although on his knees, still has his grip.

- Reach over the top of him and overhook his crotch with one hand while underhooking a thigh with the other.

- Grip your hands and lift/turn him away from the gripped thigh to his back.

Ankle spreader

● Grab his nearest ankle.

● Place your hip-side knee against the side of his near-side knee.

● Grip his ankle from the inside and spread it to the outside (not up) to put lateral stress on his knee. This will turn him to his back away from the gripped ankle.

A better angle

8
Single-leg takedowns

To the old-timers, the single leg was like the jab. Once you get it down, I think you may agree.

Single-leg pickup

● Use the same back step, level change and penetration steps as described for the double leg.

● Reach for his lead leg with your inside hand — never the outside hand since you easily can be whizzered.

● Once your inside hand grabs his lead leg, bring your outside hand around, palm down, to overhook his leg.

● You can rip him to the mat with this grip or slide your inside hand to a high crotch to finish the drop.

Another view

● Once you have his leg off the mat, move your inside hand to seatbelt his waist.

● This move is a good alternative for those who don't feel comfortable with the single-leg dives.

Single leg with inside trip

● Shoot your leg dive.

● Step your right foot behind his support foot.

● Drive into him to drop.

8.1
Single-leg
takedown
counters

A large part of beating single legs is the ability to maintain your base even while on one leg. The longer you can maintain your base, the better your options are for hooking the opponent while still on your feet. The following drill should be worked assiduously to give you confidence to hit any of the following counters.

Partner hop drill

● Lift your right leg and allow your partner to grab it at the heel.

● He should push, pull, lift and swing your leg in various directions and speeds while moving about the mat.

● Your job is to stay on a single foot, hopping for base all the while.

Drill for single 3-minute rounds per leg (it's a burner) and then return the favor for your partner.

Single-leg takedowns can be accomplished with your leg to the inside or outside of your opponent's legs, as well as with your leg caught between his legs. The first few counters are leg position specific and then it's catch as catch can.

Chin hook and chancery to roll out

● Here your leg is caught between his legs.

● Overhook his head with your right arm and gain a chin hook.

● Underhook his right arm with your left arm.

● Sit on your butt and elevate him over the top.

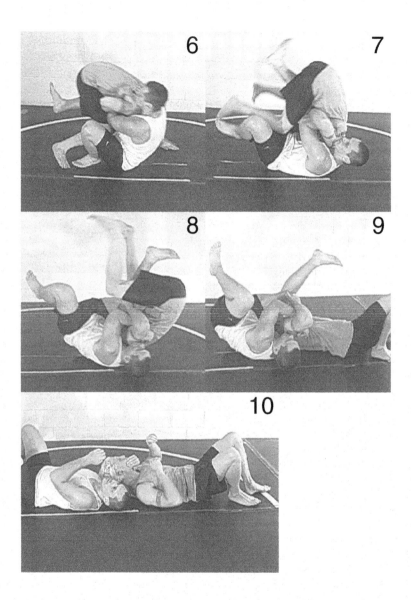

11

● He will roll and land in a top saddle/ mount with your chin hook and underhook still in place.

12

● Pull his chin and arch your back to tap.

Or use the move on the next page.

13

14

Hop out stocks

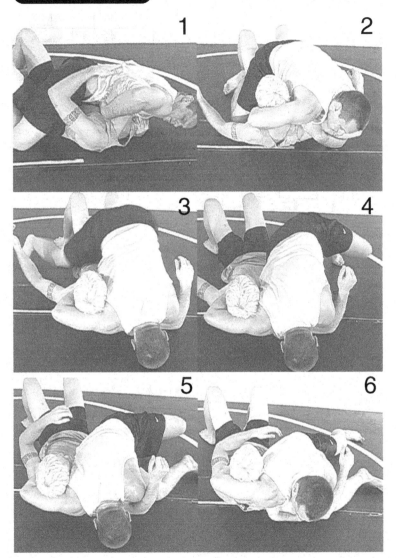

● Hit all as in the previous move. When you hit top saddle, hop out toward your underhook side and hit a sit-out toward his head to tap.

● Be careful — this is tight with a capital T.

Chin hook reap

● Your leg is caught to the inside of your opponent's body.

● Overhook his head and hook his chin with your right hand.

● Turn your caught hamstring against his hip.

● Pull his chin, hit him with your leg and take him to your left.

● Keep the chin hook and hit a sit-out as you hit the mat to tap.

● Be careful, this is a wicked drop.

Front quarter nelson

● Your leg is caught to the outside.
● Stuff his head with your right hand.
● Overhook his right arm with your left and hook a quarter nelson.

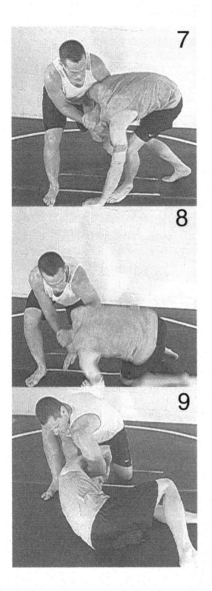

● Drive your caught leg to the mat and pressure the quarter nelson taking him to the mat.

Front quarter chin hook crank

● Setup is like the previous move, except you grip his chin with your right hand.
● Drive your caught leg to the mat while pulling up on his chin and down on his shoulder to tap.

Standing double wrist lock

● Attempt to drive your caught leg to the mat.
● Overhook his inside arm with your same side arm (right versus right).
● Weave your overhook back over the top of his forearm.

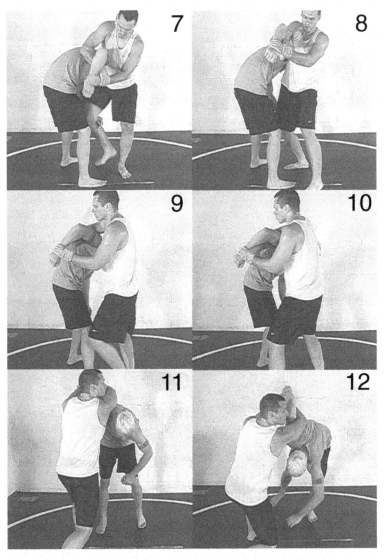

● Grip his inside arm wrist with your free hand.
● Figure-4 grip your hands and rip his arm skyward for a double wrist lock.

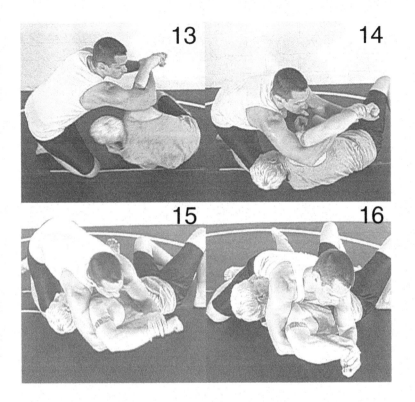

Standing switch

● Overhook his inside arm with your same side arm — attempt to have the back of your triceps against the back of his triceps.
● Now underhook his same side thigh with your overhooked arm.

● Using the back of his arm as a pivot point and his thigh as a ladder rung, turn yourself to his back.

Standing arm drag

● Underhook his inside arm with your inside hand.

● Grip his arm tightly and pull it 45 degrees and down across your body and gain a go-behind.

Single wrist lock with elevator

● Insert your arm as in the double wrist lock setup.

● Once your arm has under-hooked his forearm, turn your hand palm up.

● Drop to the mat as you insert your caught instep as an elevator into his crotch or same side inner thigh.

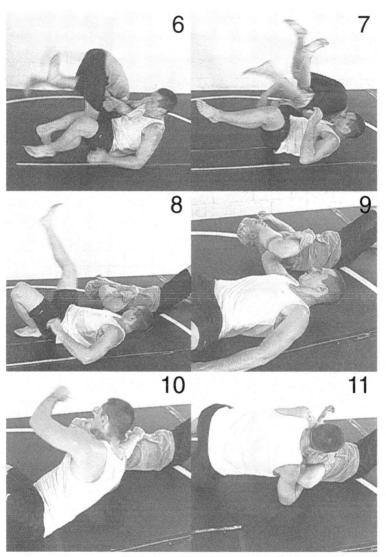

● Perform a biceps curl with your inserted arm while kicking your elevator skyward.

12

13

Drop toe hold

This counter seems a bit of a stretch, but it's there more often than you think, and quite surprising to your opponent.
● Here he has my left leg to the outside.
● I drop onto my right hip and send my right leg between his legs. My right calf blocks behind his right heel.

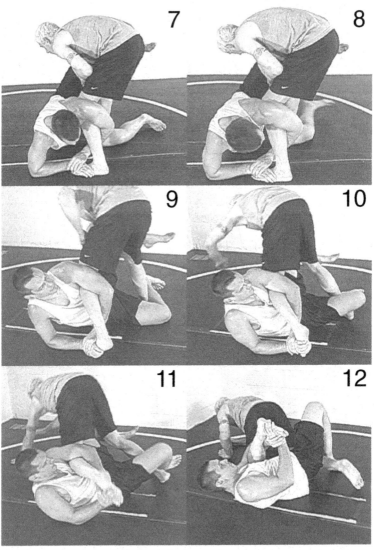

● As I drop, I grab the toes of his left foot with my right hand.
● At the same time, I overhook his left calf with my left elbow.
● The combination of dropping my weight, and banging him behind his left knee with my left elbow brings him over the top.

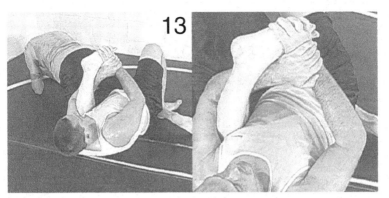

● As he hits the mat, I figure-4 grip my hands and hit a twisting toe hold.
● Detail on the twisting toe hold — It's important to twist the toes down and to the inside for maximum effect.

9
Low single-leg takedowns

These are surprising drops seen too infrequently. Master player Kazushi Sakuraba always uses them wisely.

Low single with head to the inside

This is the preferred method.

● Bang both knees to the mat and cup his heel with your inside hand. Note I position my outside forearm against his lead leg to protect against knee strikes.

● Double up on his heel with your other hand.

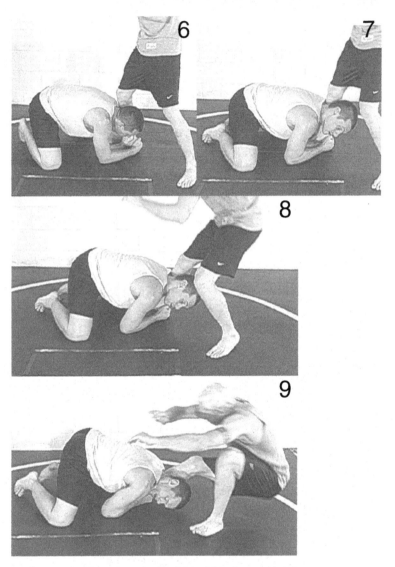

● Place your head to the inside of his leg and drive your shoulder through his shin to drop.
● Rip him to the mat with this grip or slide your inside hand to a high crotch to finish the drop

Low single with head to the outside

5 Head to the outside is not the preferred choice as stated before. It is shown because in the chaos of the fight, the second choice may be better.

● Bang both knees to the mat.
● As you descend use your forearm to gate against his attacked knee to block a potential knee strike.
● Cup the heel of his left leg with your inside hand.
● Reach your outside hand to cup.
● With your head to the outside of his leg, place your shoulder midshin and drive into him.

Low single to turn the corner to double ankle

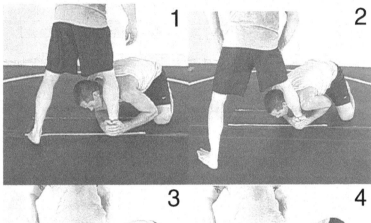

5

● Hit the low single (head to the inside or outside).

● If your opponent is able to remain on his feet, spin behind his leg and maintain your inside grip on his ankle (your inside hand will now have outside placement).

● Grab his far ankle and drive.

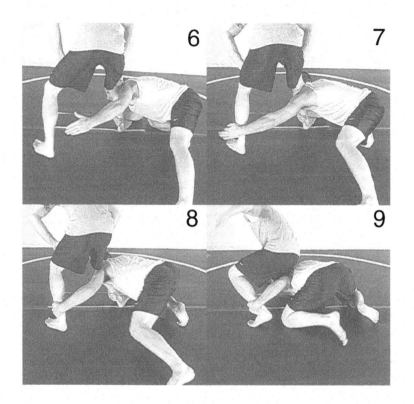

Low single to turn the corner to far knee block

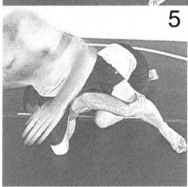

● Hit a low single.

● When your opponent blocks the move, you turn the corner, reach for his far ankle but cannot grasp.

● Reach for his far knee with what becomes your inside hand.

● Put your palm on his far knee and drive into him to drop.

9.1
Low
single-leg
takedown
counters

Good base will foil most low singles but, just in case, here are more counters.

Back sweep

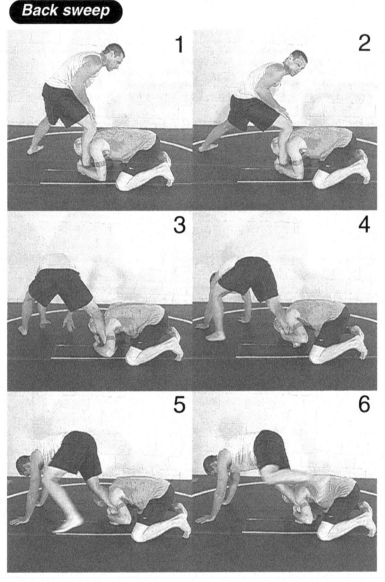

● Once your leg is caught, attempt to remain standing by posting your free leg to the rear.
● Turn to face your rear leg. You can post one or both hands on his head for safety.

● Back step your free leg over the top of his body and under-hook his crotch with your caught-side arm. If your right leg is attacked, you will underhook with your right arm.

● Overhook his crotch with your free hand. Grip your hands together and lift him to break the hold.

10
Arm drag drops

To many, the arm drag is only a setup or method to hit a go-behind (part of the arm drag's charm, yes). But the arm drag is far more useful than that. Here are a few drops to illustrate that point.

Falling arm drag and knee

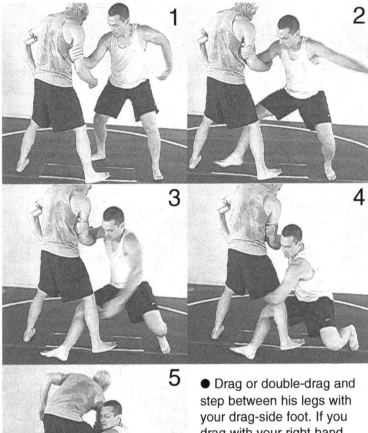

● Drag or double-drag and step between his legs with your drag-side foot. If you drag with your right hand, step with the right foot.

● Drop to your drag haunch while your free arm over-hooks his drag-side knee bringing him to the mat.

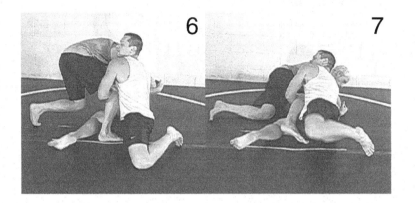

Arm drag with trip

● Hit your drag and use the arch of your drag-side foot to kick his drag-side foot out from underneath his base. This will drop him to the mat.
● Use the arch of your foot against the inside of his ankle.

Drag with inside back heel

● Hit a drag.
● Shoot your drag foot between his legs and hook a back-heel trip against his drag-side foot.
● Drive into him to drop.

10.1
Arm drag counters

The key to beating
drag drops is speed.
You must recognize
the drop and imme-
diately turn it to your
advantage. That
comes with constant
drilling.

Cross-body block for arm drag

● This is a full commitment move.
● If your right arm is dragged, step your right leg around his left leg as in an outside back heel trip.
● Drive into him to drop.

Head / thigh block

● This block demands that you take control before your arm is pulled across your body.
● Post your dragged palm on his near-side thigh or hip.
● You can post the top of your head into his chest or jaw to complete the block.

Step over counter for falling arm drag and knee

- As your opponent drops to the mat to execute this technique, step your caught leg over his body.
- Post on the mat with your free hand and knee to gain a top-saddle/mount position.

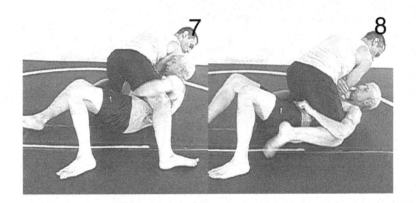

11
Collar and elbow tie-up offense

This is a common tie-up in straight submission wrestling. Do not ever agree to assume this position. Take the position and turn it into an immediate setup or beat the tie-up and look for a way to reengage.

Collar and elbow position

Good form — weight down with overgrip.

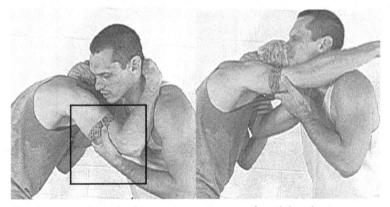

Bad — undergrip leaves you open for this shot.

● This is a variant of the over-under tie-up.
● Grab the nape of your opponent's neck with one hand (here the right).
● Your opponent does the same.
● Overhook his neck control biceps with your free hand.
● Your opponent does the same.
● Keep your elbows parallel and pointed toward the mat to prevent penetration of your defense.
● While seeking control in this position, do not allow your head to go lower than your opponent's head.

Drop duckunder

● Bang your head control side knee to the mat.

● Immediately stand up behind your opponent's head control arm for a go-behind.

Cross heel pickup

● Keep the head control and stay on the sole of your head-side foot.

● Release your arm control and bang the arm control side knee to the mat.

● Reach for his far ankle with the hand that is now free.

● By snagging his ankle, pulling his head and driving into him, you will drop him to the mat.

Near heel pickup

● Executed step-for-step as the previous except the hand reaches for the near-side ankle.

Head pull and leg pickup

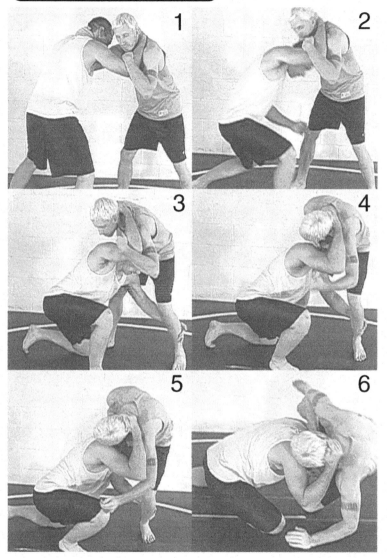

● Keep your head control and drop to your elbow control side knee.

● Overhook his far calf or knee with your elbow hand.

● Pull his head and drive into him to drop him to the mat.

Underarm sneak

● Release your elbow grip and use the palm of that hand to pop his head control elbow upward.
● Sneak your head under his popped armpit for a go-behind.

Collar and elbow tie-up offense

Arm throw-by and ankle pickup

● Release your head control and bang the head control knee to the mat.
● While doing so, toss his head control elbow to the inside with your elbow control hand.

● Reach for his head control side ankle with your head control hand.
● Drive into him to drop.

Snap down

1

2

3

4

5

● If your opponent unwisely allows his shoulders to penetrate the vertical plane drawn from his lead knee, merely snap him down to the mat.

Chin push to go-behind

● This one is useful against an opponent with a good defensive game.
● Push his chin with your head control hand.
● Underhook his crotch with your elbow control hand.

● Use the crotch grab as a ladder rung to gain a go-behind.

11.1
Collar and elbow defense

Again, an aggressive tie-up will go a long way toward stopping most of your opponent's offense at its inception.

Pancake versus heel pickup

● When your opponent drops for either a cross-heel or near-heel pickup, lift his head control arm with the crook of your elbow control arm.
● Grab his pick arm at the triceps with your other hand.
● Using your grips, turn him on his back over his pick arm.

Elbow shove versus heel pickup

A simple, yet effective block.

● Shove his head control elbow with the palm of your elbow control hand to jam his attack.

Step-behind versus underarm sneak

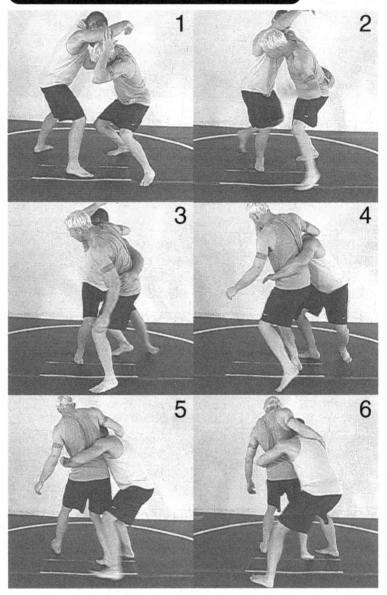

This counter is one of move recognition and speed.
● As he shoots the underarm sneak, simply turn the corner and shoot behind him.

Elbow hook versus snap down

1

2

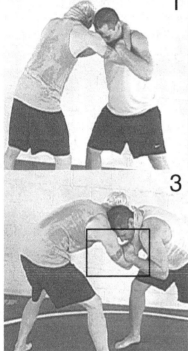

3

Keep in mind that if you are scrupulous about not allowing your shoulders to penetrate the vertical plane of your lead knee, you remove your opponent's snap down opportunities.

● As he snaps you down, grab the crook of his snap down arm to stop the movement.

Miss the crook, and you go down with the snap.

1

2

NHB / submission wrestling resources

BEST CHOICES

First, please visit my Web site at **www.extremeselfprotection.com** You will find even more training material as well as updates and further resources. Let me know if you have any questions, comments or concerns about the material in this book or about any topic regarding training.

Amazon.com

The place to browse for books such as this one and other similar titles.

Paladin Press
www.paladin-press.com

Paladin carries many training resources as well as some of my videos, which allow you to see much of what is covered in my NHB books.

Ringside Boxing
www.ringside.com

Best choice for primo equipment.

Sherdog.com

Best resource for MMA news, event results and current NHB happenings.

Threat Response Solutions
www.trsdirect.com

Same as previous. They offer many training resources along with some of my products.

Tracks Publishing
www.startupsports.com

Tracks publishes this book and its prequel and has other fine books including a couple of boxing titles.

www.humankinetics.com

Training and conditioning information.

www.matsmatsmats.com

Best resource for quality mats at good prices.

GENERAL

Equipment

Everlast
718-993-0100

Fairtex
www.fairtex.com

Ringside
1-877-4-BOXING
www.ringside.com

Magazines

Fight Sport
fightsportmag.com

Full Contact Fighter
fcfighter.com

Grappling

Books

Boxer's Start-Up:
A Beginner's Guide to Boxing
by Doug Werner

Boxing Mastery
by Mark Hatmaker

Brazilian Jiu-Jitsu:
The Master Text
by Gene "Aranha" Simco

Fighting Fit
by Doug Werner
and Alan Lachica

More No Holds Barred Fighting:
Killer Submissions
by Mark Hatmaker

No Holds Barred: Evolution
by Clyde Gentry III

No Holds Barred Fighting:
Savage Strikes
by Mark Hatmaker

No Holds Barred Fighting:
The Ultimate Guide to
Submission Wrestling
by Mark Hatmaker

The Fighter's Notebook
by Kirik Jenness and David Roy

Video instruction

Extreme Self-Protection
extremeselfprotection.com

Paladin Press
paladin-press.com

Threat Response Solutions
trsdirect.com

World Martial Arts
groundfighter.com

Events

IFC
ifc-usa.com

IVC
valetudo.com

King of the Cage
kingofthecage.com

Pancrase
so-net.ne.jp/pancrase

Pride
pridefc.com

The Ultimate Fighting
Championships
ufc.tv

Universal Combat Challenge
ucczone.ca/

Web sites

adcombat.com

extremeselfprotection.com

mmafighter.com

sherdog.com

Index

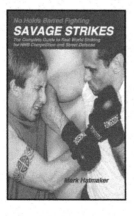

*Advanced Technique,
Tactics and Strategies
from the Sweet Science*

Mark Hatmaker
with Doug Werner

Boxing Mastery
Advance Techniques, Tactics and
Strategies from the Sweet Science
Mark Hatmaker
1-884654-21-5 / $12.95
Advanced boxing skills and ring general-
ship. 900 photos.

Mark Hatmaker is the author of *No Holds Barred Fighting*, *More No Holds Barred Fighting: Killer Submissions*, *No Holds Barred Fighting:*

Savage Strikes and *Boxing Mastery*. He also has produced over 40 instructional videos. His resume includes extensive experience in the combat arts including boxing, wrestling, Jiujitsu and Muay Thai. He is a highly regarded coach of professional and amateur fighters, law enforcement officials and security personnel. Hatmaker is founder of Extreme Self Protection (ESP), a research body that compiles, analyzes and teaches the most effective Western combat methods known. ESP holds numerous seminars throughout the country each year, including the prestigious Karate College/Martial Arts Universities in Radford, Virginia. He lives in Knoxville, Tennessee.